"Having studied, written about, and practiced corporate management for three decades, I was intrigued by Bob Briner's title and found new and compelling insights in his book. I recommend it to anyone in business."

Mark H. McCormack,
chairman, International Management
Group, and author of *What They Didn't
Teach Me at Harvard Business School*

"Bob Briner has done a masterful job on bringing to our attention the greatest leader in all of recorded history—Jesus Christ. Briner's analysis of Christ's management principles and how they are just as right today will make great sense to many business leaders."

William E. LaMothe,
chairman emeritus, Kellogg Company

"Humbling, challenging, and inspiring . . . As Christian business people, we are called to emulate Christ not only in our personal lives, but in our businesses as well. Bob Briner has just given us the ultimate handbook."

Neal Joseph,
president, Warner Alliance

"If you never read another book on management methods, this one will be quite sufficient. The timeless insights of Jesus, along with the commentary of Bob Briner, will be of immense and immediate value to anyone aiming for greater success as a manager."

Jack Kinder, Jr., and Garry D. Kinder,
well-known authors, consultants, and
speakers

"Fresh, savvy, provocative, sometimes amusing, and always practical, this is a marvelously helpful little book. Briner distills a lifetime of experience to give us lessons for leaders in all fields."

Os Guinness,
author of *The American Hour*

"Management books are a dime a dozen in our generation. . . . Volumes such as The Leadership Principles of Attila the Hun and The Art of War have found their way into the briefcases and 'war rooms' of thousands of executives in the past decade. Bob Briner has now reached up to the top shelf to retrieve the most effective management principles from the most effective motivator and mover of men and women in all history—the Lord Jesus himself."

Dr. O. S. Hawkins,
pastor, First Baptist Church, Dallas, Texas

"Bob Briner always approaches common subjects with a fresh business-man's mind. Who before, for example, has ever thought of Paul as 'the best key-man hire in history'? Maybe, Briner suggests so thoughtfully, we can better find the lessons of modern business through the precepts of a fellow who, long ago, built a pretty good company fishing for men than with all the organization charts and focus groups we depend on so much today."

Frank Deford,
author and commentator

"I thoroughly enjoyed reading Bob Briner's The Management Methods of Jesus. I read it over two evenings. The principles are true, easy to grasp, and relevant! Bob clearly presents God's wisdom and practical application from his holy Word. It is a terrific business manual. I plan to get copies for all my key managers."

Norm Sonju,
president and general manager,
Dallas Mavericks

THE MANAGEMENT METHODS OF JESUS

Ancient Wisdom for Modern Business

BOB BRINER

Thomas Nelson, Inc.
Nashville • Atlanta • London • Vancouver

Published in Nashville, Tennessee, by Thomas Nelson, Inc.

Scripture quotations are from the NEW KING JAMES VERSION of the Bible. Copyright © 1979, 1980, 1982, 1990, 1994, Thomas Nelson, Inc., Publishers.

Library of Congress Cataloging-in-Publication Data

Briner, Bob.
    The management methods of Jesus : ancient wisdom for modern business / Bob Briner.
      p. cm.
    ISBN 0-7852-7681-5 (hc)
    1. Management—Religious aspects—Christianity.
2. Success in business.   3. Jesus Christ—Leadership.
4. Executive ability—Biblical teaching.   I. Title.
HD38.B725   1996
658—dc20   95-38968
                             CIP

This book is dedicated

to our beautiful daughter,

Leigh Briner Ganton, and to her husband,

Kevin J. Ganton, a businessman

who learns from Jesus.

Contents

Acknowledgments

As with every writing project, at least with every one of mine, many people make it happen.

I want to acknowledge my editors at Thomas Nelson, Bruce Nygren and Leslie Peterson, for their very significant contributions to the book.

Dr. Os Guinness, the brilliant Christian thinker and writer, commented very helpfully on the manuscript, as did the noted business consultant, Jack Kinder.

My wife, Marty, continues to be a vital part of my writing team, as does Mary Ann Van Meter, my longtime assistant in our Dallas office.

Among the most significant contributors to this particular book are those people who have taught me about business.

My late uncle, Bill Briner, was the earliest of these.

Chuck Burr of the Miami Dolphins was my first boss in professional sports.

I worked with David F. Dixon on the planning for the Superdome in New Orleans.

Lamar Hunt was a wonderful boss as we began the modern professional tennis tour.

Robert S. Folsom, later to be a successful two-term

mayor of Dallas, guided me during my years in professional basketball.

For more than twenty years my friend and partner, Donald Dell, and I have worked together all over the world in many areas of professional sports and television.

Two splendid businessmen/craftsmen of the old school, Vance Kidwell and Maurice Daniken, have inspired and challenged me by their commitment to excellence and integrity.

All of these men, and many others, have contributed to my knowledge of business and, thus, to this book. I am very grateful to each.

Bob Briner
Greenville, Illinois
February, 1996

Introduction

Forget Attila the Hun. Where is his management legacy? You can't find it. The all-time greatest management entrepreneur is Jesus Christ. Just look at what he accomplished. By any measurement standard, the empirical evidence bears witness that the organization founded by Jesus is the most successful of all time. Longevity? Two thousand years and counting. Wealth? Beyond calculation. Numbers? Beyond counting. Loyalty of adherents? Many give their lives for it. Distribution? Worldwide, in every country. Diversification? Successfully integrated into all kinds of enterprises. Ergo, Jesus Christ reigns supreme as the greatest manager the world has ever known.

Atilla the Hun? A piker. If you really want to succeed, study, learn, and apply the management principles of Jesus Christ.

Don't get me wrong. None of this is to say that Jesus is some twentieth-century management guru—replete with formulas, slogans, and seminars for revolutionizing business life. For one thing, he is so much more than that. Too many people have already pressed Jesus into too many molds, trying to make him conform to their idea or ideal. But this is what impresses me and what I hope will impact you: Take the life and teaching of Jesus out of any mystical or spiritual context, and you will see that it is packed full of wisdom highly relevant to my world and yours—the world of business. See what you think.

Have a Plan

It is amazing how few companies have a master plan by which they chart their course and measure their progress. Even fewer individuals have constructed a plan for their lives with short-term, intermediate, and long-range goals. This is a fundamental mistake.

Jesus had a plan and adhered to it unfailingly. This is a major reason for his success. He knew where he was going, and he went there. Nothing deterred him. Knowing that the culmination of his plan had to be accomplished in Jerusalem, and even knowing that the ultimate sacrifice would be required of him there, he set his face like a flint for Jerusalem, say the Scriptures (Isa. 50:7). Jesus was resolute. Whatever the consequences, he would go to Jerusalem and carry out his plan.

A fundamental management principle then, both for individuals and for organizations, is to have a plan to which you are deeply committed, and then to set out with

A plan puts you in charge of your energies and activities.

determination to accomplish it. Without a plan, you have nowhere to go, nothing toward which to direct your energies. Without a plan, you can only react to circumstances. A plan puts you in charge of your energies and activities. You become proactive, not reactive.

Be Prepared

In a cosmic sense, Jesus' preparation was without a beginning. It was forever. Even in an earthly sense, Jesus prepared for *thirty years* before beginning to execute his plan.

As finite beings, we don't have thirty years to formulate our plan, but Jesus' example is, as always, a good one. To insure maximum effectiveness, the fullest realization of our plans, we must commit to the necessary preparation.

In my forty years in business, I have rarely felt overprepared. I have often felt severely underprepared, and the results have borne out that feeling. Inadequate preparation produces inadequate results.

Jesus based much of his approach to accomplishing his plan on his understanding of the Old Testament. He had a foundation of knowledge upon which to base his actions, and he executed brilliantly. To succeed, we must do the same thing.

Many young people come to our company who

Inadequate preparation produces inadequate results.

want to be in the television business. In television, writing is the foundation for everything. An axiom in our business says, "If you can't first put it down on paper, you can never put it up on the screen." Yet so many of the young people who come to us have not mastered even the fundamentals of grammar, the basics of the English language. They haven't prepared. They won't succeed.

Jesus powerfully taught us about preparation, both by his own perfect example and by his teaching. Many of the parables he used to explain his principles admonish us to be well prepared. For example, the parable of the foolish virgins, who were caught without oil in their lamps when the bridegroom came and thus missed the wedding, teaches us about adequate preparation. So also does the parable of the servants, who did not perform their assigned tasks and were not ready to meet their master upon his return. They thought the master would be away a long time, so they wasted their time and received the master's wrath when he returned unexpectedly.

Whether you're laying the foundation for a career, launching a product, or making a presentation, there is no substitute for preparation. Give it the necessary time and attention. Jesus did. His amazing success is a testimony to its importance.

Choose Your Own Associates

One of the biggest mistakes corporate boards and other hiring entities make is to select a leader and then saddle him with a staff not of his choosing. It doesn't really matter how good that staff is. If the leader didn't choose them, and if *they* didn't choose him, the odds for failure are enormous.

If you want a manager to do a job for you, give him the right tools. And remember that a manager's most important tools are the people who work for him.

If you are considering taking a management position, one of your prerequisites should be the right to build your own immediate staff. If your superiors don't want you enough to give you that opportunity, then maybe they don't want you enough to make it worth your while. Managing is difficult enough without the additional handicap of a "poorly fitting" staff. The outside forces arrayed against you are formidable enough. The last thing

---

Remember Jesus' example.
Choose your closest associates, and allow
those you hire to do the same thing.

you need is a staff of "leftovers," some of whom, no doubt, feel they should have had your job.

If you're doing the hiring, don't go through the trouble to find and attract the best possible talent only to hamstring him with a staff he does not want and vice versa. Give your managers the freedom to choose their key people and, in an orderly way, bring those people in to replace those who will be moving on.

If you are being considered for a management position, don't jeopardize your reputation and future opportunities by agreeing to a position in which you must keep the present staff. It rarely works.

Jesus, of course, chose his own disciples and did so carefully. True, one of the twelve betrayed him, but I wish I had been successful in selecting the right employee eleven out of twelve times. I would be a lot richer and more successful than I am! History shows that Jesus did an extraordinary job of selecting his staff. And, if you understand his plan, you will know that even Judas, his betrayer, was part of it.

Remember Jesus' example. Choose your closest associates, and allow those you hire to do the same thing. It is the best way to increase your odds for success.

To Fill a Key Spot, Pull Out All the Stops

One of the biggest mistakes our company has made is not going all out to get a key employee for a crucial spot. If we had looked to Jesus and followed his example, we wouldn't have made that mistake.

Even with the twelve great men Jesus had in place (Matthias replaced Judas), he saw the need to add one more top-level person to his organization. To say he went all out to get his man would be an understatement.

As Saul of Tarsus was traveling along the road to Damascus, Jesus literally knocked him to the ground and blinded him with a light from heaven. He identified himself and told Saul, who would become the great apostle Paul, what he must do. Now that is aggressive recruiting!

I think it is safe to say that Paul's enlistment in

When the position is really a key one, and the person in sight is exactly right for it, go full speed. Get your man or woman.

Jesus' cause is one of the most brilliantly successful hires in the annals of human organizational history. Paul became an executive recruiter, an organizational fund-raiser, an opener of new branches, and, most important, a faithful and prolific disseminator of the organization's message. He told Jesus' story better, more often, and more successfully to more people than anyone else. Through his great letters, he is still telling it.

Paul was the ultimate "key man," and his "hiring" has many lessons for those who are trying to build organizations today.

First, when there is a key spot to fill and you have identified the right person for that spot, *go get him* (or *her*). Don't let the normal constraints of salary schedules, protocol, or convention deter you. Whatever you do, don't ask yourself, "What is the least I can offer this person and still get him?" On the contrary, ask yourself, "What is the most I can afford to offer this person to show how much I want and need him?" You can't blind the recruit with a light from heaven, but you should dazzle him with what you *can* offer. When the position is a key one, and the person is exactly right for it, go full speed. Get your man or woman.

Second, do not pass up a key person because of a misguided concern about what your current employees might think. Our company has sometimes made the mistake of not going after a top executive because we knew we would have to bring him in at a level above any of the current staff, and we were afraid this might offend them. That is counterproductive thinking. Chrysler's decision to bring in Lee Iacocca to run the corporation was the best thing not only for the company but for the executives who were passed over for the job. He saved Chrysler and made everyone associated with the company more successful.

All of Jesus' original disciples—particularly Peter, James, and John, who were with Jesus from the beginning of his ministry and had shown some concern about their own status—might well have resented both the way Paul was recruited and the almost immediate status he assumed within the organization. The original disciples had spent three tough years with Jesus, traveling the dusty roads of Palestine, sleeping wherever they might find themselves, and going through the excruciating ordeal of his arrest, trial, and crucifixion. They might well have said, "No one ever came to *us* with a light from heaven. Who is this guy Paul anyway?"

But they didn't, probably because Jesus' call to "Come follow me" was just as impressive and precious to them as a blinding light from heaven. (This then is another management principle to learn from Jesus: Tailor your recruitment methods to the person you hope to attract. A simple "come" was sufficient for Peter, the uncomplicated fisherman beside the Sea of Galilee. But the proud, educated, pharisaical Saul needed to be knocked flat by a light from heaven.)

After some suspicion and testing, Paul was fully integrated into the organization.

Again, when there is a crucial spot to fill, do whatever it takes, in an honorable way, to fill it with the best person.

Third, Jesus taught us not to overlook our competitors in our search for the best people. Paul was the most energetic, the most vocal, the most feared, and the most effective of those arrayed against the fledgling organization established by Jesus. He was, in fact, its chief competitor. Jesus recruited him and made him a key man in his own building effort.

When you hire a quality person from your competitor, you accomplish two things: You strengthen your organization, and you weaken the competition. With Paul in the Church, he was no longer a threat to the Church. Jesus was a brilliant organizational strategist. Learn from him.

Teach, Teach, Teach

A public service announcement says, "Be a teacher. Be a hero." We might well say to corporate managers, "Be a teacher. Be a success." Most of the legendary corporate giants, from Henry Ford to Tom Watson to Ross Perot, have been persistent and motivational teachers. They may well have received their inspiration from Jesus Christ, the greatest of all teachers.

Jesus was often called *rabbi,* which means *teacher,* and he taught constantly. His teaching brilliance is revealed in the New Testament books of Matthew, Mark, Luke, and John, which are full of his remarkable insights. His ability as a teacher is also demonstrated by the success of his pupils, his disciples, as they carried out his plans and programs.

Great corporate leaders don't hide in executive suites, plotting strategy. They find ways to teach, to inculcate those around them with their business ideas and ideals. Be like Jesus. Be a teacher. Be a success.

Be like Jesus. Be a teacher.
Be a success.

Practice Private Communication

Jesus taught in all kinds of situations. He spoke to large audiences, to dinner party attendees, and to church (synagogue) groups. However, his most important and meaningful teaching was reserved for small groups, particularly with his most intimate confidants, Peter, James, and John. When he wanted to be absolutely sure his point was made, he went one on one.

Jesus' earthly brother James (not the disciple) had understandable difficulty believing in his sibling's divinity until the two of them spent time alone together. After that, James became a leader and directed the activities of Jesus' organization in Jerusalem. James was eventually sentenced to death for his belief in Jesus. Now *that* is effective teaching.

It is important that corporate leaders give both quality time and quality instruction to their most trusted aides. It will pay great dividends.

When he wanted to be absolutely sure his point was made, he went one on one.

Establish Authority

Jesus did not run a democratic organization. Not once did he call for a vote on the course that should be followed. He was in charge. He based his authority on the Scriptures and on the commission he had from his Father. Even he submitted to a "higher" authority—"Not My will, but Yours, be done" (Luke 22:42).

In this day, when nonauthoritarian leadership is lauded at every turn, it is important to note that no successful organization is ever built or maintained without strong ultimate authority. Ask any of the great corporate leaders. Was there ever any doubt who was boss when Iaccoca was at Chrysler, Watson at IBM, Perot at EDS, or Buffet at Berkshire Hathaway? Who ran Wal-Mart? You can bet Sam Walton did.

Participatory decision making may be okay to an extent, but only when there is real, ultimate, final author-

Know the extent of your authority
and exercise it.

ity at the top. Be sure there is no doubt about where the buck stops in your organization. Know the extent of your authority and exercise it. Establish and maintain authority.

Insist on Absolutes

From pontificating pundits and tweedy talk show academics who have never met a payroll, we hear that it is not politically correct to insist on absolutes. From truth to justice, all things are relative, they say. It's how you feel about it that counts. "Two diametrically opposing thoughts can both be true," they say, "because there is no absolute truth."

Please don't try to run your business by this nonsense. Jesus insisted that some things are true and others false, that some things are right and others wrong, that some things are good and others evil. He even insisted that there is only one way to be reconciled to God, and that one way is through faith in him. Talk about tough! Talk about dogmatic! Jesus never equivocated. Sincerity didn't count with him if what you believed was sincerely wrong.

A lack of absolutes can lead to all kinds of corporate problems, from petty thievery to major crimes. It leads to shoddy products and shoddy practices in the marketplace.

A lack of absolutes can lead to all kinds of corporate problems, from petty thievery to major crime. It leads to shoddy products and shoddy practices in the market-place. "I didn't think I was doing anything wrong" is a common defense of everything from manipulating stock to adding extra nicotine to already lethal cigarettes to building cars with dangerous fuel tanks.

As a company and as a manager, teach the right way, insist on the right way, be an example of the right way to do business. Follow Jesus' example.

Watch Your Timing

As you would expect, Jesus' timing was always perfect. It was never haphazard and always had significance. Because his timing was so exquisite, each particular event had greatly enhanced impact.

It was no accident that he timed his first public miracle to happen at a wedding, thereby setting his seal on marriage and emphasizing its importance. Timing his entry into Jerusalem and his subsequent crucifixion and resurrection—both of which happened during the Passover celebration—was one of the most brilliantly played strategies of all time.

During Passover, Jews from every nation came to Jerusalem. There they witnessed the amazing events triggered by Jesus. More important, many of them were convicted of their sin by the inspired and compelling preaching of Peter and returned to their homelands as converts. Thus, when Paul and the other apostles began

Because his timing was so exquisite, each particular event had greatly enhanced impact.

to fan out from Jerusalem to spread the word, they found allies waiting for and welcoming them. They didn't have to start from ground zero in building local organizations. Brilliant timing. Tremendous results.

Timing should always be a consideration in your corporate planning. Major announcements should be timed for maximum impact. New products should be introduced at the most opportune time. Where appropriate, tie them into significant anniversaries and public holidays.

Timing should also be a consideration in releasing the inevitable bad news every organization has from time to time. When can you disseminate it to the public at the least cost to the image of the corporation?

Timing was key in the success of Jesus. Make it work for you too.

Handle Corruption Immediately

Warren Buffet, the legendary investor and chairman of Berkshire Hathaway, was more critical of Solomon Brothers's slowness in acting on knowledge of the bond-trading scandal within the company than of the scandal itself. Evidently top management had known of the problem for some time before they took the necessary corrective action. Waiting almost cost them the company, and it exacerbated the damage.

The management at Kidder Peabody, an old-line, prestigious Wall Street investment house, made almost the same mistake, failing to move decisively when they first learned of illegal activities within their company. Kidder may never be the same.

Both managements could have profited by Jesus' example of dealing with the money changers in the temple

---

When there is clear, irrefutable evidence of any kind of corruption within the corporation, move immediately to handle it. Never, never try to cover it up.

in Jerusalem. When he observed the activities of these extortionists and usurers in God's house, he didn't call for a committee meeting. He didn't put the problem on the agenda for the next board meeting. He didn't call in the spin doctors to discuss how best to handle the situation. He immediately and forcefully drove the slime-balls out. This is a powerful lesson for everyone in management.

We have not always followed this approach in our own company. Too often we have waited too long, dilly-dallying around and shuffling our feet with our hands in our pockets when confronted with clear and irrefutable evidence of "bad people doing bad things" within our company. We almost always could and should have acted sooner with a much more positive effect.

Jesus' example is a forceful one. When there is clear, irrefutable evidence of corruption within the corporation, move immediately to handle it. Never, never try to cover it up. It doesn't work, and those who participate in the cover-up are generally dealt with more harshly than the original perpetrators. The first reflex is almost always to see if the problem can be corrected without swift and forceful action. That reflex almost always serves us and our organizations poorly.

Now, acting forcefully and quickly does not mean going off half-cocked. Jesus' decision to drive the goons out of the temple wasn't based on rumors or unsubstantial reports. He knew what was going on. He saw it. Gather your facts, then act. Don't put it off. Get it over with and move on.

Don't Sugarcoat

Jesus told his disciples over and over about the terribly difficult days ahead for himself and for them. He didn't promise an easy path.

Unrealistic expectations damage employee morale, perhaps as much as any negative circumstance you can imagine. This is almost always cited when an employee goes into an unproductive funk or quits. "I thought it was going to be different" or "I was told I would be doing something else" are statements most often heard during an exit interview. Most people can handle most situations when they have been honestly prepared to face them.

When trying to recruit a new desirable employee, it might be tempting to paint an overly glamorized picture of the job and of your company. Don't do it. Obviously you should present the job and the company in the best possible, *honest* and *realistic* light, but don't oversell. Don't

---

Let your associates know exactly what lies ahead for them.

overcommit. Don't promise what you cannot deliver. You might gain new employees by putting on rose-colored glasses for prospects, but you will lose them pretty fast when reality fogs up the lenses.

Certainly you should allow prospective employees to see the possible upside, but they should know as much as possible about what will be required of them to reach the sunny climes of success. The ones you really want will appreciate the challenge and your honesty.

Let your associates know exactly what lies ahead for them. If it is long hours, lots of travel, belt-tightening, let them know. Let them step up to the challenge of tough times. Lead them into the future with their eyes wide open, ready to tackle what lies ahead.

Get Away from It All

Even with all Jesus had to accomplish during his short stay on earth, he still took plenty of time off.

He made sure he had time alone for prayer and reflection. He got his sleep. There were times when everyone else was awake but Jesus was sleeping.

As always, he is a great example for us. It may seem politically savvy and the macho thing to be thought of as a go-go guy, never resting, never getting away. But a well-rested executive always accomplishes more than a tired, stressed-out executive. Take your vacations. Real vacations. Ones in which you truly do get away from the office.

My friend and partner, Donald Dell, one of the legendary high-energy, hard-driving executives of our industry, always schedules a few weeks, spaced throughout the year, during which he truly gets away. To remove even the temptation to "check in," he often goes to places

Take your vacations. Real vacations. Ones in which you truly do get away from the office.

where there are no phones. He comes back refreshed, energized, and ready to get back into the action with gusto. He learned the benefits of this kind of scheduling as a world-class tennis player, captain of the United States Davis Cup Team, and veteran of marathon negotiating sessions.

As important as it is for you to get away, it is just as important for your subordinates. A smart executive will make sure that in their zeal to please, to advance, or to make just one more deal, his employees don't drive themselves so hard they have a flameout. Maybe if the top executives at Fidelity had insisted that Peter Lynch take more time off, he would still be picking stocks for them and earning the company tens of millions of dollars. Lynch was an amazing business phenomenon who built Fidelity's Magellan mutual fund into one of the largest and most successful in history, before walking away an early victim of burnout.

Jesus valued time away, time alone. You should too.

Field-Test Your Staff

I f your staff is going to do its best for you and the company, and if you are going to do your best for them (which should also be one of your management goals), from time to time you will need to let them test themselves out in the field, away from you and your supervision. Give them specific tasks, and then let them go do them. If you have taught them well and given them clear and specific instructions, these will be times of learning and growing as well as times of advancement for your enterprise.

Jesus did this with great effect when he sent out twelve disciples one time and seventy another. He sent them two by two, which is also a technique we should consider. He gave them very specific instructions as to what they were to do and warned them of the adversities they would face. Again, these are important principles to learn. Don't be vague or general in making assignments. Be as specific as the situation allows. Also, share with

---

They still had lessons to learn and growing to do, but that field experience, away from the "home office," was of tremendous value.

your people, to the full extent of your knowledge, the difficulties they are likely to face in the field. Send them out as fully prepared as possible. Jesus did.

When the seventy returned to Jesus, the Scripture says they "returned with joy" (Luke 10:17). They found, out in the field, out with the adversaries, out away from supervision, that "it works." And Jesus, their teacher and leader, was so thrilled by their accomplishments that the Scripture says he was also full of joy. The disciples were never the same again. They still had lessons to learn and growing to do, but that field experience, away from the "home office," was of tremendous value.

Practice Good Public Relations

My longtime friend and business partner, Donald Dell, was an advance man for Robert F. Kennedy during his presidential campaign, which was cut short by his tragic assassination. Donald has taught me a lot about what a good advance man does to prepare the way for the one for whom he is working. The most successful advance man ever, and the prototype for all to follow, was John the Baptist.

John was so great because he knew his role. His statement—"He [Jesus] must increase, but I must decrease" (John 3:30)—should be the motto for all public relations people. Too many begin to think they are the stars, when it should always be the enterprise and its executives who are the stars.

John also excelled in the use of words. He spoke some of the greatest, most profound lines in all of Scripture. Get a wordsmith to tell your company's story.

Too, John's timing was excellent. He was in the

You need to tell your story. Your company needs to tell its story and the story of its products and services. Do this well.

right places at the right times. This is a must for a first-class public relations executive. If someone is always late, misses deadlines, doesn't understand time zones and their relationship to news, and is unable to seize the moment, he is not the person to handle your public relations and publicity.

John demonstrated that good, solid, *true* public relations is a worthwhile and honorable undertaking. In our day public relations has sometimes been given a bad name by those who have seen it as a shallow, hype-filled undertaking. But, as John practiced it for Jesus, and as you should consider employing it in your business, public relations is a valuable activity that, when practiced with integrity, is useful for all concerned.

You need to tell your story. Your company needs to tell its story and the story of its products and services. Do this well. Take great care in selecting the one who will represent you to your various publics.

John the Baptist was, without a doubt, the most carefully chosen advance man of all time. He literally was conceived and born for the role. You and your company should also take great care in selecting those who will tell your story. Set a high standard for them. Truth should always be the first requirement for any public relations effort. Have your people tell the truth, tell it well, and in a timely way, and they will benefit you and your company. They should learn from John the Baptist.

Get Good Logistical Support

A misconception many people have, and one I had for many years, is that Jesus traveled around Palestine, fulfilling his plan, with only a small band of followers. This is erroneous. A careful reading of the Gospels reveals that a significant number of people accompanied him. As we learned earlier, at one time he sent out seventy men, two by two, to test them in the field. There is no reason to think the seventy included everyone who was with him at the time. There could have been many more.

Several passages in the Scriptures refer to "many women" who were in Jesus' traveling company and who followed him all the way to Jerusalem and to his death on the cross. We know in another instance there were 120 of his followers gathered in a large room.

Now, Jesus was devoting his time to teaching, doing the essential work only he could do. Not once do we read

> *Make sure you are as free as possible to do the things only you can do—the things you were hired to do and the things upon which you will be judged.*

of him dealing with the enormous logistical operation that must have been necessary to meet the needs of his people.

This, of course, is ripe with lessons for us. First of all, it is absolutely essential that managers not get bogged down in logistical details. I know a CEO of a multinational company who allowed himself to get involved in choosing desks for secretaries, allotting office space for very junior people, and other minutiae. This not only drove his people crazy, it kept him from doing the things only *he* could do.

Jesus did not get involved with details. He used his staff for those. Jesus did the things only he could do.

Don't get trapped into handling small details. Make sure you are as free as possible to do the things only you can do—the things you were hired to do and the things upon which you will be judged.

Learn a Little Humility

The image of the insufferably arrogant business executive is too close to reality for comfort. In my own career, I have seen examples of unbelievable arrogance on the part of top business executives. I am sure I have displayed an unseemly amount myself.

I have also seen this arrogance come back to haunt those who came to believe in their own invulnerability. As this is being written, one of the legendary despots of the publishing industry finally, after years of abusing subordinates and lesser lights in his industry, got his. His bosses (ultimately everybody has a boss) got fed up with his arrogance and summarily dismissed him. As the *Wall Street Journal* said, "He still doesn't get it." This guy's company was making money. He was lionized in many quarters, but his arrogance caught up with him. Now he is history.

You would think in a business as volatile as televi-

Don't fall into the trap of arrogance. Not only is it unseemly, it is bad business.

sion, even the top executives would know how precarious is their perch. Because I have been in the business so long, I have seen dozens of television execs come into power, become mesmerized by their corporate sway, become unbearably arrogant, and then fall when the inevitable shifts knock them aside. My partner and I used to keep a list of the guys who would not return our calls when they were on top but would begin calling us frantically when they were wiped out and looking for friends.

Don't fall into the trap of arrogance. Not only is it unseemly, it is bad business. One way to combat it is to keep a picture in your mind of Jesus Christ, God's perfect son, kneeling before ordinary men, his own disciples, and washing their feet. With this picture in mind, it is pretty hard to be arrogant.

Share the Glory

To me, among the most touching and telling parts of the Gospels are passages in which Jesus praises John the Baptist. He was lavish in his public praise of this devoted servant. John was eventually martyred for his devotion to Jesus.

I was a member of a college trustee board once in which the president of the college was not a brilliant academician or administrator, but he had one of the most successful tenures in the history of the institution. I think one of the reasons, perhaps even the principal reason he was so successful, was that his faculty and staff would do almost anything for him, would go to great lengths to make him look good. And one of the reasons they did this was that he constantly gave them all the credit. He looked for ways to praise them. At every board meeting and on most public occasions, he made sure his people

Praise those who work for you.
Do it publicly.

were lauded, and they made sure they went the extra mile for him. A great deal for both of them.

Remember Jesus and John the Baptist. Praise those who work for you. Do it publicly. It is good business.

Say "Thanks"

Golfing great Jack Nicklaus is legendary for saying thanks. This began back in the early days of his career when he would stay in private homes during tournaments. Some people still prize the note of thanks he wrote to them back in those days. As he became a superstar in golf and in business, Nicklaus continued to look for ways to express his gratitude, and it has paid off in many ways for him.

You will note that Jesus always gave thanks for food before he ate. He was exceedingly thankful to his Father for the power his disciples demonstrated when he sent them out two by two. His appreciation for the demonstration of love by the woman who bathed his head with expensive oil and who washed his feet with her tears is another fine example of his gratitude.

In business, really in all of life, it is impossible to say "thank you" too many times. Do as Jesus did. Say it often.

In business, really in all of life,
it is impossible to say "thank you"
too many times.

Stay in Touch with Real People

Jesus touched lives in every level of society. He had many discourses with the societal leaders of his day, but he chose some of the most humble of men as his closest associates. He traveled with, spoke to, and cared for people of every class.

Corporate managers need to be sure they don't lose touch with real people leading real lives. The higher up the corporate ladder you go, the stronger the possibility of isolation. In the early days of our company's effort to build professional tennis, one of the investors was a wealthy young man from Dallas. We were discussing with him the scheduling of events and noted that August would be a good time for an event in Dallas. He was incredulous, saying, "There is nobody in Dallas in August. Everyone is in Europe." Now, I had lived most of my life in Dallas and had never been to Europe in August. Dallas seemed just as full of people in August as at any

Corporate managers need to be sure they don't lose touch with real people leading real lives.

other time. But to this young man, because he and his friends went to Europe in the summer and didn't return until fall, "everyone was in Europe."

Stay in touch with real people. They are your customers and employees. Jesus did. You should too.

Be Responsive

Nowhere in any of the gospel accounts do we find Jesus telling someone to wait. He never said, "I'll get back to you" or "Don't call me, I'll call you." He never put anyone on hold.

Jesus took care of business on the spot. He answered questions, turned water into wine, fed the multitudes, and healed the sick of body and soul instantaneously.

We, of course, don't have the perfect insight and miraculous power of Jesus, but we should follow his example to the greatest extent we can. Unresponsiveness has all too often become the norm in American business. It seems that fewer and fewer executives return phone calls or answer their mail in a timely way. This presents a wonderful opportunity for those who follow Jesus' example of responsiveness. By returning phone calls and answering correspondence promptly, and by getting peo-

He never put anyone on hold.

ple the answers they need as soon as possible, you will begin to stand apart from run-of-the-mill managers. Once again the example set by Jesus turns out not only to be good sense but good business too.

Don't Neglect Public Speaking

Jesus, of course, was a masterful public speaker. He drew large crowds everywhere he spoke. Any list of great public discourses would have to include the Sermon on the Mount. It is a classic of both poetic beauty and powerful content.

American business executives have a largely well-deserved reputation for being dull, boring, tiresome speakers. This is true both when they speak to the troops in-house and when they address outsiders. Too many fail to use the platforms their positions give them both to inspire and to inform. Instead, they often use stale, statistically heavy speeches with no life and no fire. This is a mistake. Because of their positions, businesspeople often have captive audiences. They tend to think that because people show up to hear them, they are fascinated by their presentations, even if they give a routine reading.

Don't fall into this trap. Find yourself a peer who

Too many executives fail to use the platforms their positions give them both to inspire and to inform.

is willing and able to honestly critique your performances. Hire an outside consultant if necessary. Make sure he knows you want to get *better,* not *flattered.* Make sure your opportunities to speak in public are not wasted for your company or for *yourself.*

Cut Your Losses

On several occasions, the Gospels tell of Jesus' leaving a place where he knew he was not wanted—like in Gadara, where the people asked him to leave, and he did. He instructed his disciples to do likewise. They were to leave any city that did not welcome them and "shake the dust of those cities" off their feet.

This provides a helpful business insight: Don't let pride or stubbornness keep you in a market in which you don't belong, or with a product that is not going to make it, or in a business alliance that is not going to work out.

In our own company we have learned this lesson the hard way, and it has cost us a lot of money. It has also cost us a lot of forward momentum in profitable areas—areas where we could have done even better had we cut our losses on inherently bad deals and invested that time and money in the profitable areas.

This is not about giving up and rolling over at the

Don't let pride or stubbornness keep you in a market in which you don't belong.

first sign of trouble or difficulty. It is about carefully analyzing losing situations and making sure you are not refusing to pull the plug because of stubbornness or pride.

Cut your losses. Jesus did.

Learn How to Rebuke

Rebuke is an archaic word. We don't hear it or use it much in contemporary society. However, there are occasions when a good old-fashioned rebuke or "correction" should be the action of choice. A rebuke should obviously be used sparingly and judiciously, but there are times when it is appropriate.

Jesus effectively demonstrated how to use a rebuke. He saved his harshest reprimands for the insufferably proud and arrogant Pharisees. And surprisingly, for his closest disciples when they too displayed pride and arrogance.

For our purposes, it is probably better to focus on the rebukes Jesus gave his disciples. The first and most obvious lesson is that, on occasion, even those nearest to us in business might need a rebuke. As was the case with Jesus and his team, it will most often be when pride and arrogance get in the way of worthy goals and objectives.

As my partner and I look back over long business

Rebukes are reserved for those you care about and respect most.

careers, we can see times we could have helped our company *and* helped our employees with a stern, old-fashioned rebuke. We recall situations in which we should have "pulled that person up short" when he stepped out of line. On these occasions, the arrogance and personal agendas grew to a point where ultimately a corrective action was needed anyway—a more severe one than would have been called for had we used a well-meaning rebuke early on. Most often, we have seen those same employees go on to similar failures in other situations. We could have helped them and helped ourselves with a corrective rebuke.

Another important lesson to be learned from Jesus' rebukes is that they don't always engender disloyalty. Not one of the disciples Jesus rebuked ever left him. Even Peter, to whom Jesus said, "Get behind Me, Satan!" (Matt. 16:23, the sternest rebuke I can imagine) never left. In fact, those Jesus rebuked most harshly became his biggest success stories.

The lesson is that Jesus had built the kind of relationship with his disciples that could survive and even *profit* from a stern rebuke. We must be sure that we have invested enough in a close business relationship to know that a rebuke will be profitable, even though painful. The person receiving the rebuke must know that there is a reservoir of goodwill and respect that is larger and more permanent than the rebuke. In fact, it should be obvious that your rebukes are reserved for those you care about and respect most.

Follow the example of Jesus. Use a rare rebuke well.

Beware of Sycophants

The higher up the corporate ladder you go, the greater the temptation to let yourself be surrounded by "yes-men." There is a great temptation to believe their baloney. This is always dangerous.

In the first place, though you may be blind to it, your business associates recognize sycophancy for what it is—ego boosting run wild—and they will lose respect for you. Also, the higher you go, the greater your need for solid, truthful, *critical* advice and information. This kind of information is vital.

I have seen business situations in which no one was willing to tell the top person the bad news he or she desperately needed to hear. The chief gets only the rosiest of pictures until the bad news becomes so overwhelming it can no longer be hidden. By that time, the battle is often lost and the situation irredeemable.

You need to be the kind of leader who appreciates and rewards those who will tell you the truth, no matter how distasteful that truth might be.

An executive is only as good as the information he has—good and bad. You need to be the kind of leader who appreciates and rewards those who will tell you the truth, no matter how distasteful that truth might be.

Corporate boards are also susceptible to the good-news-only syndrome. This is particularly true in the non-profit sector. Board members are too often brought in, wined, dined, and entertained and given only the brightest of pictures as to the state of the enterprise. Don't allow this to happen. Whether you serve on a profit or nonprofit board, you have significant fiduciary responsibility, and often significant liability. Insist on the whole truth—good and bad.

You should also remember that your board service often has a direct bearing on your own business success. Many top corporate executives have reached the high point in their careers by the quality of service they deliver on boards—both on for-profit and on not-for-profit boards. If you serve, do a good job.

The easiest thing to do as an outside director is to take all the reports of the corporate executives at face value and never ask questions. A rule of thumb is that if you are only getting good news, you are not getting the whole picture. No enterprise complex enough to require an outside board operates without problems and failures. As a board member or trustee, be sure you know about them. Don't let the staff "yes" you to death.

I know of a board where this happened. The president of the enterprise put together a docile executive and business affairs committee who never asked the tough questions and who never reported anything but good news to the full board. The rest of this board sat fat, dumb, and happy for several years. When the president retired, all the bad news came to light, revealing that the institution was precarious financially. They had to scramble to keep it afloat. Don't let this happen to you.

Again, Jesus provides the greatest of all examples. He continually dismissed insincere flatterers, but accepted honest praise graciously. We need to do the same in all our relationships, but particularly in business.

When the rich young ruler came to Jesus calling him "good," Jesus brought him up short because he knew the man was not a sincere worshiper. The same thing happened with the teacher of the law who told Jesus, "Teacher, I will follow you wherever you go."

Jesus stopped the hypocritical Pharisees cold by quoting Isaiah: "These people . . . honor Me with their lips, / But their heart is far from Me" (Matt. 15:8). But when people came with honest, sincere praise, he could not have responded more positively.

In business as in life, we need to be sure that we discern the difference between honest praise and insincere, self-serving, sycophantic flattery. We need to do as Jesus did: Seek the truth in all things and in all people.

Be a Servant

Throughout the formation of his organization, the Church, Jesus repeatedly emphasized servanthood, the idea that the way to succeed is to put others first. Many hard-charging business types see this approach as sentimental, even otherworldly—something for another time and certainly for an activity other than business. The conventional wisdom is that to be number one, you must take care of number one.

The reality is, however, that the surest way to success for a business executive is to put his employees and his customers first—in effect, to become a servant to them, meeting their needs. The annals of business are full of success stories in which the model of "others first" was a surefire formula for success. The mystery is that so few "get it." So few are willing to learn from either Jesus or from contemporary organizational examples.

The surest way to success for a business executive is to put his employees and his customers first—in effect, to become a servant to them and meeting their needs.

Now it is important to point out that being a servant to your employees and your customers does not mean "giving away the store" or going soft-headed and namby-pamby. Not at all. That's no way to serve your employees or your customers. To meet your employees' and customers' needs, your company must be successful. Only successful companies survive to serve.

This kind of servanthood does require an attitude that asks, "How can I best take care of the needs of my employees and customers in the context of a growing, thriving business?" It certainly does not mean you sell your products below cost or put all potential profits into salaries and bonuses. That would be ridiculous, self-defeating, and ultimately threatening to your organization.

In business, the opposite of the servanthood model is the one that, if articulated, would be, "Let's pay these guys as little as possible and charge our customers as much as possible for the products we make as cheaply as possible so we can make as much as possible." This is not a pathway to success.

To succeed, use the Jesus model. Take good care of your employees and your customers. When Jesus said in Matthew 23:11, "He who is greatest among you shall be your servant," he made a statement by which any business can live and thrive.

Discourage Position Jockeying

Jesus' disciples, exhibiting very human tendencies, constantly worried about their respective ranks in the hierarchy. Matthew, Mark, and Luke all record arguments among the disciples about which of them would be greatest in the kingdom of God. The mother of James and John, probably at her sons' urging, even asked Jesus to grant her a favor—honored positions for her two sons.

Business executives often observe their subordinates spending much of their valuable time arguing, plotting, and positioning *themselves* for advancement rather than advancing the *corporate* cause. It is not at all uncommon for those in such a group to even sabotage one another's projects to keep a rival from looking good. Obviously this is counterproductive.

Jesus did not put up with this kind of nonsense. He cut all the arguments short with the statement, "Let him who would be greatest be the servant of all." And he

---

"Just do your job. Serve the employees
below you and your customers,
and you will do all right."

told James and John's mother that she didn't know what she was asking. A paraphrase of Jesus' comments for business leaders would be, "Just do your job. Serve the employees below you and your customers, and you will do all right."

Today's managers should be alert for similar maneuvering among subordinates and nip it in the bud with the same kind of response. However, for this to be effective and fair, executives must be sure they are evaluating real results and are not being misled or manipulated. A good manager, a successful one, will know who is producing and who is only talking about producing.

Be a Fruit Inspector

During more than thirty years in business, I have been richly rewarded by people I have hired. Unfortunately I also have many failures sprinkled through my hiring record. Even after using sophisticated evaluation tools and the experts' advice, our company has lost a great deal by hiring employees who have not been successful. Jesus has some help for those of us who are charged with hiring employees.

In the seventh chapter of Matthew, he tells us that "every good tree bears good fruit, but a bad tree bears bad fruit" (Matt. 7:17). This seems obvious, but its truth can be lost in the hiring process. An applicant may be physically attractive, come from a good school, have an excellent academic record, score well on aptitude tests—and still be a disastrous hire.

Two examples come readily to my mind. I know two men who are handsome, well-groomed, well-spoken,

---

"Every good tree bears good fruit,
but a bad tree bears bad fruit."

and attended prestigious schools. Yet they consistently continue to perform less than spectacularly in business. The amazing thing is that people continue to hire them for prestigious and demanding positions. They are hired because they are handsome and have impressive credentials, not because of their record.

When you are hiring, look long and hard at the results the person has produced. Follow the advice of Jesus: Be a fruit inspector.

Stop Worrying

Jesus had a lot to say about worry. He saw it as both counterproductive and evidence of a lack of faith. He said firmly not to worry at all.

Now there is a world of difference between planning and worrying. We are admonished to plan carefully and even to "sweat the small stuff." Planning and paying attention to details are positive activities because we can make positive things happen as a result.

Worry, on the other hand, is by definition useless fretting about things over which we have no control, and it produces no positive results. Many successful businesspeople recount how they concentrate intently on their businesses during working hours but never worry about them during the evening. This is consistent with Jesus' teaching. In Matthew 6:34 he says, "Therefore do not worry about tomorrow, for tomorrow will worry about its own things."

There is a world of difference between planning and worrying.

Avoid Grandstand Plays

Throughout his earthly ministry, Jesus was constantly asked to perform spectacular feats. Satan was a persistent tempter in this regard. And the Pharisees kept after him to produce a "sign in the sky" to demonstrate his power and divinity. Jesus never fell for it.

Obviously he did many wonderful and powerful things, but always with a purpose, always to help others, never just to draw attention to himself. Certainly, the miracles he did perform helped to build the faith of his followers, but they had already come to him because of his words, his message.

Businesspeople are often tempted by the grandstand play, usually to inflate an already oversized ego. Making grandiose claims for a product not yet fully developed or buying an expensive corporate toy, such as a corporate jet, that the company really cannot afford are classic business grandstands. I'm sure you can think of your own examples.

Businesspeople are often tempted by the grandstand play, usually to inflate an already oversized ego.

I know one investor who has a rule: "If you see a CEO on *Lifestyles of the Rich and Famous,* don't buy his stock." Donald Trump is the master of the grandstand play, always making a dramatic entrance, always pictured in the tabloids. Most Americans would not recognize Warren Buffet if they met him face-to-face. But his stock sells for $20,000 a share. No grandstand plays for him.

Be like Jesus. Resist the temptation to make grandstand plays.

Be Fair to All, Generous Where Appropriate

In our company, we have sometimes failed to reward one person sufficiently for fear of what some other employee might think. The reasoning goes this way: "If we give Bill the bonus he really deserves, Max will hear about it and be upset that he didn't get a bonus as well."

Max was being paid all that he had been promised and had not performed as exceptionally as Bill. If we were being fair to Max, we shouldn't worry about what he thinks of Bill's compensation. To do so is to cheat Bill out of his rightful reward.

Jesus taught this principle clearly in the parable about the landowner who paid the worker he had hired last (who had worked a much shorter time) the same as those who had worked all day. When confronted about this by one who had worked all day, the landowner re-

---

If we were being fair to Max, we shouldn't worry about what he thinks of Bill's compensation.

plied, "Friend, I am doing you no wrong. . . . Take what is yours and go your way. I wish to give to this last man the same as to you. Is it not lawful for me to do what I wish with my own things? Or is your eye evil because I am good?" (Matt. 20:13–15).

Be fair to all. Be generous when generosity is merited.

Be a Risk Taker

Anyone who thinks that Jesus would advocate only a stodgy, ultraconservative business philosophy has never read or understood the parable of the talents as recorded in Matthew 25:14–30.

In this famous and forceful story, Jesus describes how a man going away on a journey entrusted sums of money to his workers to handle for him while he was away. He entrusted the most money to the ones with the most ability. Those who invested the funds and multiplied them earned the man's praise. However, the one who buried the funds entrusted to him and returned only the amount he was given received the man's wrath.

The lesson of this parable is that we are to multiply our assets by investing them wisely. Jesus clearly knew that there are risks involved in investing, but the servants who doubled the money entrusted to them are put forth as good examples to us all. The servant who buried the

As corporate managers entrusted with our stockholders' assets, our job is not to preserve capital but to grow it.

money entrusted to him was called "wicked" and "lazy." He was told that the least he could have done was to put the money on deposit in a bank so it could have earned some interest.

As corporate managers entrusted with our stockholders' assets, our job is not to preserve capital but to grow it. This means investing in new procedures, new products, new markets, and new people. It means taking prudent risks.

In the business world, as in our personal life of faith, we are called to put our assets and abilities to good use.

Take Care of the Children

Jesus was the ultimate pro-family leader. He continually gave special attention to children. During one incident he was greatly displeased when his disciples hindered people from bringing their children to visit him (Mark 10:13–14).

The wise and successful corporate leader will do all he can to take care of the children—his, those of his employees, and if his products are used by children, his customers.

Among the most important and *productive* things a corporate leader can do for the children of his employees is to do all he can to see that mothers and fathers spend time with their children. A corporate executive has only so much control here. There is no way he or she can mandate quality time with the kids even if plenty of time off is allowed. However, a corporate executive can be sure that families and children are not shut out and shut off by the kind of demands placed on mothers and fa-

> *Nothing angers the public more than a business that is not mindful of its responsibilities to children.*

thers. Managers can create a climate that honors and promotes balance.

There are also lots of ways companies can let their employees know that their children are important to their employers. These range from big things such as company-sponsored college scholarships for the children of employees to small things such as recognizing the achievements of children in the corporate newsletter.

Nothing angers the public more than a business that is not mindful of its responsibilities to children. Just ask those hapless executives who tried to pass off colored water as apple juice.

A major children's food company with an honored brand name was practically wiped out and several of its executives fined and imprisoned when they sold what was basically colored water, calling it apple juice for children. Both the public and the courts come down hard, as they should, on any business or businessman seen to be exploiting children.

Remember what Jesus did. "He took [the children] up in His arms, laid His hands on them, and blessed them" (Mark 10:16).

Pay Your Taxes

One of Jesus' most remembered statements is: "Render therefore to Caesar the things that are Caesar's, and to God the things that are God's" (Luke 20:25). This is not only a pithy saying, but it also provides clear instruction for us. Among other things, it means that we are to pay our taxes.

I know of no one who enjoys paying taxes—personal or corporate. Enjoyment is not the issue. Obedience is. Obedience to the law of the land, as well as to God's law.

I am always amazed by the number of stories in the *Wall Street Journal* about both individuals and companies virtually ruined by not paying their taxes. These managers are usually highly educated, with batteries of accountants and tax attorneys at their beck and call. Yet they deliberately try to get away without paying taxes. They get caught, and their careers and sometimes their lives are ruined. Some serve prison sentences.

Don't pay any more taxes than you have to. But pay all that you owe. "Caesar" and God will both be pleased.

Get the best tax advice available. Don't pay any more taxes than you have to. But pay all that you owe. "Caesar" and God will both be pleased. And you will sleep better.

Let Your Results Speak for You

At one point John the Baptist sent his associates to ask Jesus a key question, the most important one he would ever ask. It is recorded in Luke 7:20: "Are You the Coming One, or do we look for another?"

Jesus could have answered indignantly. He could have set the record straight. Instead, he said, "Go and tell John the things you have seen and heard: that the blind see, the lame walk, the lepers are cleansed, the deaf hear, the dead are raised, the poor have the gospel preached to them" (Luke 7:22). Jesus let his actions speak for him.

In your corporate life, there will be times when your credentials and experience are questioned. When this happens, as much as possible, cite results. Tell what you have done, not what you think of yourself. Don't be defensive, but let your record speak for you. Ultimately it will anyway.

Tell what you have done, not what you think of yourself.

Don't Cast Your Pearls Before Swine

Corporate gadflies and provocateurs are the bane of many corporate executives. At stockholders' meetings, it is incumbent on the one presiding to answer every question from a stockholder, no matter how ridiculous or provoking. Learn to do this with poise and equanimity.

However, outside those highly structured, legally called meetings, corporate executives need to exercise discretion and common sense about "cast[ing] your pearls before swine" (Matt. 7:6). Everyone deserves to have his question considered, but answers are required only to cogent questions asked with goodwill.

Top executives of a large corporation could devote much of their time responding to questions, comments, and criticisms that are really not worth the investment.

> *Top executives of a large corporation could devote much of their time responding to questions, comments, and criticisms that are really not worth the investment.*

They must be careful that *their* time is given only to that which merits attention.

Again, Jesus said, "Do not give what is holy to the dogs; nor cast your pearls before swine" (Matt. 7:6). That is good advice for the corporate setting.

Be an Inspirational Leader

Did not our heart burn within us while He talked with us on the road, and while He opened the Scriptures to us?" (Luke 24:32).

This beautiful passage from Luke testifies to the charismatic appeal of Jesus. People were drawn to him and to his cause and were amazed because he "taught with authority." In today's language, we would say, *"He really knows what he's talking about."*

The basis for all Jesus' teaching and the thing that gave him "authority" was his knowledge of the Scriptures. The Scriptures provided the historical and philosophical base for his enterprise, the Church. His success in articulating his vision is empirically demonstrated two thousand years later in the enduring strength of his Church.

None of us can hope to have the charismatic appeal of Jesus. Our enterprises can never have the cosmic and eternal consequences of his great organization. But our

Be a cheerleader as well as a coach.

business affairs are important to us *and* to him. He cares about our success and failures. One of the ways to build a successful enterprise is to use Jesus' example and to speak with authority, to know what you are talking about, and to communicate that knowledge with passion. The corporate executive who thinks inspiration is a by-product of the bottom line, production figures, and dry-as-dust statistics misses one of the great lessons of Jesus. It's also a lesson taught by the lives of many of the great builders of business throughout history. They succeeded to a large extent because they believed so fervently in what they were doing and were able to instill some of that fervor in their associates. From Thomas Edison to Lee Iacocca, the great leaders of American business "taught with authority." They not only knew what they were talking about, they developed a style of delivering their information that emulated the "burning" Jesus kindled in the two men on the road to Emmaus.

So whether your corporation's particular endeavor is turning out widgets or is some other more glamorous enterprise, you need to know and share the stories about its history and its importance in the lives of the people it serves. If you can't tell your organization's story with enthusiasm to employees and prospective employees, to investors and prospective investors, and to customers and prospective customers, you probably should seek employment elsewhere.

My dad spent his entire working life in the business of manufacturing paint. This brings to mind the cliché that is a synonym for boredom: "about as interesting as watching paint dry." Yet my dad was passionately involved with his work; he understood its role in people's lives, and he could discourse on it so eloquently and enthusiastically that he made the paint business interesting and compelling for those of us who walked with him. Now well into his eighties, he still enjoys sharing his stories of a business some would see as ultimately bland and uninteresting, and I still enjoy hearing them.

Be sure you know the history of your business and how it benefits people. Know why your business matters. Be able to discuss it with feeling and fervor. Be a cheerleader as well as a coach.

Prune for Productivity

Both through his actions and his teachings, Jesus demonstrated that he expected his followers to be fruitful and productive. He was unequivocating on this.

In the powerful and profound fifteenth chapter of John, we read these words of Jesus: "I am the true vine, and My Father is the vinedresser. Every branch in Me that does not bear fruit He takes away; and every branch that bears fruit He prunes, that it may bear more fruit" (John 15:1–2).

As managers entrusted with the health of an enterprise, we must constantly cut and prune. People, departments, and branches that are not productive *must* be cut away. This should never be done in a casual or cavalier manner. The people involved should always be seen as important and valuable, but they must be evaluated by their productivity. Just as Jesus said that the unfruitful fig tree and the unfruitful branches of the vine should be

As managers entrusted with the health of an enterprise, we must constantly cut and prune.

done away with, the unproductive parts of businesses must be phased out and closed down.

Equally important is Jesus' lesson that every branch that bears fruit must be pruned to enable it to bear more fruit. The history of business is replete with enterprises that enjoyed great initial success but then grew complacent. They were content with past glories, and they eventually collapsed, victims of management that didn't continue to "prune" for even greater productivity.

Don't Try to Serve Two Masters

When considering the various jobs to be done and the available personnel to do them, executives are often tempted to "split up" an individual by assigning him or her to two or more supervisors as well as two or more job tasks.

This is easy to do on an organizational chart. The reality is, however, that such an arrangement almost never works and almost always results in bruised feelings, intramural squabbling, and poor performances. At least one of the tasks, sometimes both, will be done at less than the optimum level, and there is a good chance you will have at least three unhappy employees on your hands.

In Matthew 6:24 Jesus tells us in no uncertain terms: "No one can serve two masters; for either he will hate the one and love the other, or else he will be loyal to the one and despise the other." It has taken us a long time to learn this lesson in our company. All too often, in a misguided effort to hold personnel costs down or to

---

No one is happy. The job is done poorly—if at all.

find a viable position for an otherwise inviable employee, we have made the mistake of assigning someone to several tasks and to multiple supervisors. It's exactly like Jesus said: The employee is invariably more successful in one part of the assignment than in the other and, enjoying that success, gravitates more and more to it and to the praise of his or her supervisor in that area.

The other supervisor, knowing he is getting short shrift and seeing the task not getting done properly, becomes more and more unhappy. He or she begins putting pressure on the employee with divided loyalty and begins to complain to the other supervisor. No one is happy. The job is done poorly—if at all.

If it becomes absolutely necessary to assign an employee to two decidedly different tasks, at least have the person report to a single individual who oversees his or her performance in both areas. This arrangement is less than ideal, and the supervisor will have to be both vigilant and skillful to see that each task is given proper time and attention. Here, too, the employee will almost invariably be more successful in one task than the other and will inevitably want to give that task more time and attention. Staying on top of the situation is a constant battle for the supervisor, and his people skills must be sharply honed to succeed.

We need to take all Jesus' admonitions seriously. This includes the one about the impossibility of serving two masters.

Remain Calm in the Storm

In every episode recorded about the life of Jesus, when outside forces created tumult, he remained calm. (There were times, of course, when he created the storm, *was* the storm. Then he was anything but calm, but this type of reaction was a rare occurrence and part of his plan. The most famous example of this is when he stormed through the temple, driving out the money changers and con artists who were preying on the people.)

When the storm raged on the Sea of Galilee, his disciples had to wake him from a peaceful sleep before he arose to calm the waters. When various people rushed to him with dire news of sickness or death, his comments were always calming and reassuring and his actions deliberate and helpful. Even in the most tumultuous hours of his life, during the events leading up to his crucifixion, while others fell apart emotionally, Jesus remained calm.

The most graphic example of this was Jesus' behav-

Being calm does not mean being detached. You can be calm and still be fully engaged and actively involved.

ior in the Garden of Gethsemane just before his arrest. When a mob armed with clubs and swords came to arrest him, Peter excitedly drew his sword and cut off the ear of one of those seeking to take Jesus into custody. Instead of reacting with angry words, Jesus immediately calmed the situation.

In the life of almost every corporate manager and executive, there will be times when you feel an "armed" mob is coming after you and your company. Labor unrest, product safety breakdown, critical material shortages, takeover attempts, and the dreaded cash-flow crisis are examples of those kinds of times. That is when the effective leader remains calm and provides effective, positive, reassuring leadership.

Most of us don't inherently have the serenity and assurance to automatically project calm in the face of the storm. That's a characteristic we must cultivate. The most important prerequisite is to recognize the need for this calm spirit. It is amazing how many executives still think that cursing, shouting, and generally running amok are the appropriate and best responses to a crisis situation.

A word of caution, however: Being calm does not mean being detached. You can be calm and still be fully engaged and actively involved.

Next to recognizing the need for calm, the most important thing is to plan for tough times. The wise executive will have carefully drawn crisis plans appropriate to the various challenges that might arise. He will also have a crisis team in place, and each member of the team will know his role. This kind of planning helps insure calm all around.

Another useful but often neglected calm-producing activity is prayer. This, like some of my other suggestions, might seem a little mystical to the average business manager. But even spiritual skeptics have noted the empirical evidence of the calm that prayer produces. History, too, is full of anecdotal evidence of the power of prayer to help in times of crisis. It is not coincidental that Jesus spent the hours just before his arrest in prayer.

Be like Jesus. Be a calm and effective leader, even in the eye of the storm.

Settle Disputes Quickly

So much time and productivity are lost because business disputes are allowed to drag on unsettled. This is true of both intracompany and intercompany disputes. A good manager will have and enforce a policy that calls for immediate face-to-face resolution of disputes within the company, as well as guidelines for resolving all disputes outside the company as soon as possible. To allow them to linger, grow, and fester is always counterproductive. Advantage is almost never gained through delay.

Jesus said, "Agree with your adversary quickly" (Matt. 5:25). He indicated that if legal proceedings are approaching, the parties should try to come to an agreement before the dispute reaches court.

Disputes within a company are usually more harmful than those between companies. Employees battling one another damage both individual and team effective-

> *One attribute of an effective executive is the ability to be a peacemaker, to be a catalyst for reconciliation.*

ness, and the bad blood usually spills over and infects a wide circle of other employees.

Managers should remember another of Jesus' statements from the Sermon on the Mount: "Blessed are the peacemakers" (Matt. 5:9). One attribute of an effective executive is the ability to be a peacemaker, to be a catalyst for reconciliation. An executive who can give the kind of leadership that promotes a peaceful company will be a successful executive. This doesn't mean that healthy competition between individual employees or groups of employees should be squelched, but the competition should promote productivity and progress—not destroy them.

Some executives practice a management style that is conspiratorial in nature and that pits employee against employee. I have never known this style to produce either a happy or an exceptionally productive work environment. As always, Jesus' way is the best way.

Sometimes, in order to be a peacemaker and to settle disputes quickly, managers may have to dismiss one or both involved in a dispute. When differences are irreconcilable, even when confronted openly and honestly, it may be necessary for someone to leave the company so as not to have a contentious workplace. If this is the case, so be it. Just be sure that all those involved have had a fair hearing. If the dispute is dealt with quickly, the negative fallout should be minimal.

In disputes with parties outside the company, the

same imperatives apply. Try very hard to settle them as quickly as possible. An executive with enough authority to settle the dispute should meet as soon as possible with a person of like stature on the other side. If these kinds of meetings are not productive, then the next step is to seek arbitration. Going to court should be the last resort.

Eat with the Troops

When you consider how many things of paramount importance were conveyed by Jesus to his disciples while they were eating, it is impossible not to note the significance of food and mealtimes in the building of his organization.

Sharing meals together creates a special atmosphere for building relationships. The Last Supper is the most obvious biblical example of this, but it is not the only one. On many occasions, mealtime was special in Jesus' work with his disciples. Food and eating were a part of most of the occasions when Jesus appeared to his disciples after the resurrection. These were particularly important times of sharing his thoughts and vision, and Jesus wanted to maximize their impact. Eating with his disciples helped do that.

Managers neglect these lessons to their detriment. There is a temptation to have lunch at your desk in order to move more paper, to eat with a customer to increase

---

Meals with those who work with you and for you should be a part of your schedule.

sales, or to eat with your peers from other companies for fun and fellowship. There is nothing wrong with any of these options, and they should be a part of a well-considered schedule. But meals with those who work with you and for you should also be a part of that schedule.

On one particularly compelling occasion, after his resurrection, Jesus prepared breakfast for the disciples, who had been fishing all night. What a sight this must have been for them to see their risen Lord, there on the shore, preparing a meal for them. What a time of fellowship and learning most certainly followed.

If you barbecue, cooking a meal for your staff and serving them would not be a bad idea. If you don't, consider other ways you might feed the troops.

But do eat with your troops. It will make them better soldiers.

Evaluate Constantly

J esus constantly evaluated his disciples. He wanted to see if they were really grasping all that he was trying to teach them. He did this by asking them questions. This continued throughout his time with them on earth.

Most often he was disappointed with their answers and found that he had more teaching to do.

Don't take communication for granted. Make sure those working for you understand both the company's goals and the methods to reach those goals. Do this by asking questions. Managers often assume that everyone is on the same page and that everyone agrees on both the goals and the ways to reach them. In reality this may not be the case. By asking questions and having your people articulate the answers, you will be able to determine the extent of their understanding and identify the areas that need to be retaught.

Evaluation should not be a once-in-a-while kind of

Make sure those working for you understand both the company's goals and the methods to reach those goals.

thing but a constant, ongoing practice. Questions should be one of your most used management tools. As noted business consultant Jack Kinder says, "When you ask right questions—when you monitor and measure what matters—performance always improves."

Share Corporate Lore

Management gurus from Warren Buffet to Tom Peters have noted the importance of corporate culture to the success of an enterprise. Corporate culture is built primarily on the stories of both corporate success and corporate failure. Those stories need to be told and retold, and their truths need to be applied to situations currently facing a company.

Jesus did this in two ways: He told Old Testament stories, using the Scriptures to great effect, and he used parables to communicate some of the most important lessons he needed to share.

Frito-Lay, the giant snack-food arm of Pepsico, has a legendary distribution system. *Legendary* is the right word. Many writers have noted that it is by repeating stories of the lengths to which Frito-Lay's delivery men have gone to get even the smallest order to the most remote customer that responsive distribution continues to be inspired.

Successful managers tell "war stories" over and over as a way of teaching how things are done at this company.

Other companies have their own stories upon which their corporate culture is based. Successful managers tell these "war stories" over and over as a way of teaching how things are done at this company.

Make sure you know the legends, lore, and parables of your company. Use them to build a corporate culture that will result in success.

Take the Narrow Path

Jesus' admonition to enter the narrow gate with the few rather than go the broad way with the many has great wisdom for those in business. Almost all business successes to some degree are based on this instruction.

Going against the grain, finding a unique way to do something, or seeking out and occupying a special niche are all part of this kind of thinking. Success in business almost always depends on differentiating what you make or what you do from your competitors. In business, the narrow way is the way to success.

Intel basically produces only one thing, a tiny computer chip. Yet this relatively new company may well become the single most profitable company *in the entire world.* Its founders carved out a niche, a narrow way.

Nordstroms, the fast-growing upscale department store, has carved out its narrow way by delivering better

Those managers hoping for success should look for ways to set themselves apart in positive ways from those who walk blithely down the broad way.

service than its competitors. All the big department store chains offer essentially the same merchandise, but at Nordstroms customers have come to expect and receive better, more personal service. This sets the company apart and makes it special and successful.

Every great business success has in some way found a narrow way, a way others could not or were not willing to go.

The narrow way should be a business goal for individuals as well as businesses. Those managers hoping for success should look for ways to set themselves apart in positive ways from those who walk blithely down the broad way.

Spending more hours on the job than anyone else or working harder than anyone else is not necessarily the way to do this. Try caring more about quality than others do. Try serving both your customers and those who work for you better than anyone else does. Try having the most congenial work environment in your company. These are narrow ways that will lead to success.

Serve Families

The first miracle Jesus performed was done at his mother's request. Another of his early miracles was the healing of Peter's mother-in-law. It is instructive to note how often he did things for a family member of one of his followers—someone's brother, someone's son, someone's daughter. To show that he cared about those close to him, he showed that he cared about those close to *them*. This is a powerful and valuable lesson.

When you hire someone, you may not want to accept the fact that you have hired his or her entire family in the sense that his or her best performance will only be forthcoming when there are no distracting family problems.

You can help build loyalty and productivity by genuinely caring about an employee's life outside the company. This does not mean being paternalistic or insinuating yourself into situations where you have not been invited. Jesus only went where he was asked to go. It

> *When you hire someone, you may not want to accept the fact that you have hired his or her entire family.*

does mean that you display an empathetic attitude that will encourage your associates to come to you for advice and help.

But you need to be discerning. Help when you can with such things as an internship for a son or daughter, or a letter of recommendation to a college admissions officer. With issues that are out of your area of expertise, you should show real care and concern and then point individuals to a source of professional help. When you can provide the help through such things as a few days off, a leave of absence, or a temporary salary advance, you need to carefully consider what will be for the ultimate good of the employee and the company. These things—at the right time, in the right amount, and with the right attitude—can produce great good for all. They must, however, be done with discretion and discernment, as an expression of genuine caring, and in the context of building productive relationships with all your employees.

Prepare for Tough Times

There is one thing you can count on in business and in life—tough times will come. The wise manager prepares for them. Many companies that once had great success, even over long periods of time, were wiped out when the tough times came because they were not prepared for them.

Jesus continually prepared his followers for the tough times. Over and over he warned them that the trials would come, both to him and to them. Some of his sternest rebukes were issued when the disciples refused to heed his warnings about the difficult days ahead.

Jesus' preparation paid off to an extraordinary degree. From the stoning of Stephen to the crucifixion of Peter, the toughest of all tough times, martyrdom, came to all the disciples. Yet because of the way Jesus had prepared them, they persevered. They triumphed. And their enterprise, the Church, didn't fall apart when the tough times came. On the contrary, after going through

The high-flying front-runners without reserves and without a plan for the tough times do not survive.

the traumas, sorrows, and persecutions, the Church emerged stronger and more vibrant than ever.

It is axiomatic in business that those enterprises that are prepared to stand the inevitable tough times and can survive the shake-ups will eventually prosper and even dominate a business segment. The high-flying front-runners without reserves and without a plan for the tough times do not survive. Their bones are strewn across business history.

In business, it is necessary to prepare for both the general tough times and the specific periods of crisis that are likely to come to your enterprise. All economies are cyclical. There will be downturns, recessions, and maybe even depressions. Financial reserves and an orderly plan for downsizing during these times are often keys to survival. Too, there are likely to be times of crisis specific to your business. Both a crisis plan and a general damage-control plan need to be in place.

Jesus, showing his great wisdom, invested a great deal of his most precious time in teaching and planning for the tough times. So should you.

Stand Up for Your People

When outsiders criticize your staff, they are indirectly criticizing you. So when you stand up for your people, you are building loyalty and camaraderie while also defending yourself.

Jesus always defended his disciples. When the Pharisees criticized them, he knew he was the ultimate target of their scorn. It must have engendered a great feeling among the disciples to have the Master come to their defense.

When your people are doing their best, when they are honest in their efforts to serve you and the company, stand up for them in the face of outside criticism. When you cannot defend them and their performance against outside attack, either you or they need to move on.

This does not mean you should deny mistakes. But it is possible to acknowledge an honest error without denigrating the person unfortunate enough to have made

When you stand up for your people, you are building loyalty and camaraderie while also defending yourself.

one. "That was a mistake in which we all participated. John, who is a great colleague, just happened to be the one who was on the front line when it happened" is the kind of statement that serves well.

Jesus demonstrated great loyalty. Follow his lead!

Set Priorities

In many ways, the entire life and ministry of Jesus was about setting priorities and adhering to them. When he said, "Let the dead bury their own dead," Jesus spoke to the need not to be distracted from the real and most important goal, even in those emergency situations that claim our attention (Matt. 8:22). And perhaps his most famous and telling statement of all, "Seek first the kingdom of God and His righteousness, and all these things shall be added to you" (Matt. 6:33), brilliantly sums up the entire message of Jesus. In other words, get your priorities straight and everything else will fall into place.

I am struck by how many times even top managers, cited in *Forbes, Fortune,* and the *Wall Street Journal* are quoted as saying something like this: "Our problem is that we have lost focus," or "We need to remember why we are in this business in the first place," or "We turned our company around by getting back to the basics," or

> *A universal number-one priority for all companies should be "serving customers and employees."*

"We needed to reorder our priorities." In other words, even the captains of industry have trouble with priorities—setting them, remembering them, and making sure that *everything* they do reflects them.

Usually setting priorities is not the problem. The problem comes in getting distracted from them, going off on tangents, and letting "good" things crowd out the "best" things. A good manager will make sure he and his team revisit the company priorities on a regular basis and subject all that is done to rigorous scrutiny, vis-a-vis the company's real goals. If an activity or an effort does not relate directly and positively to the priorities, it needs to be terminated. Or the priorities need to be consciously changed. This should be done rarely and with the greatest of care.

One of the most common examples of how companies lose track of their priorities is in their advertising. CEOs become enamored with clever, trendy, even award-winning advertising—until it dawns on them that although people remember and admire their advertising, it does not sell their products! Then, if they survive, they go back to basic advertising, which might seem pedestrian or mundane but sells their product. This, after all, is why they are in business. Awards and the praise of the trendsetters are nice, but they cannot compare to a growing bottom line or an increasing dividend and stock price. Paying constant attention to priorities is the way to success.

Every company will have priorities unique to it and its business. I would suggest, however, that a universal number-one priority for all companies should be "serving customers *and* employees." This seems to be so basic, but it's often forgotten, neglected, or put aside to accomplish some secondary goal. When this occurs, the company always suffers.

An all-too-frequent example of this is when a management team focuses all its energies on producing a dramatic, short-term earnings increase. "Let's make the fourth quarter look so good that everyone will notice," is a way this is often articulated. The real priorities of serving customers and employees are forgotten. Quality, service, and the long-range health of the company suffer. They're sacrificed on the altar of something that is not a real priority.

As always, Jesus has the right idea for our individual lives *and* for our businesses. And the good news is that his priorities for our lives are not incompatible with solid, practical, profit-making priorities for our businesses.

Set priorities. Keep them in mind. Always.

Prepare for Your Successors

Almost from the first day he was with them, Jesus told his followers that he would be with them only a short time. From time to time they argued with him about the limited tenure he described, but he continued to reiterate that his time with them would be very limited.

Even though it is almost a cliché in business school to say that a good manager's first duty is to prepare for and train his successor, the reality is that few do. Even faced with the obvious fact that *everyone* will either be promoted, demoted, fired, move to another company, change careers entirely, retire, or die, very few managers prepare for these eventualities properly and in a timely, systematic, measured, unself-conscious way. In fact, talking about a future where the one in charge will no longer be around is almost a taboo. It's like death—everyone knows that it will come, but no one wants to discuss it.

In most business situations, a great pretense is lived

Executives seem to perpetuate the myth that they are immortal and that their presence is permanent.

out. It is the pretense that in spite of the fact that most executive tenures are relatively short, and *all* are finite, the manager in question will be at his post forever. In most companies it would be thought unseemly to say, "Well, Bill, retirement is not too far down the road for you. What have you been doing to see that your department (division or company) moves forward smoothly after you're gone?" Or "Bill, given the uncertainties we all face, what sort of plan is in place should something, good or bad, happen, and you are no longer here?" Executives seem to perpetuate the myth that they are immortal and that their presence is permanent.

Get real. Recognize that you will, sooner or later, move on. Discuss your eventual leave-taking openly and frankly with your staff. Have a plan in place in case you are unexpectedly no longer around. Have a plan in place even if the transition is more orderly and planned.

Jesus' plan for transition was the most successful in history. He had prepared his followers well, openly discussing his eventual departure. His associates did not want to see him go, but they were forewarned. They performed beautifully after Jesus was taken from them, pushing the program forward to unimagined success.

Jesus planned well for his succession. So should you. Your company and your associates deserve it.

About the Author

Bob Briner is the president of ProServ Television, Inc., one of the world's leading producers and distributors of sports television. He has more than thirty-five years' experience in international business and marketing. He is also an Emmy-winning producer and has written for publications around the world, including *Sports Illustrated* and the *New York Times*. He is the author of *Roaring Lambs* and *Squeeze Play* and serves on the boards of civic and charitable organizations.

Briner lives in Greenville, Illinois with his wife, Marty.